DEVOTIONS *for the* FAMILY

No. 3

DEVOTIONS
for the
FAMILY

No. 3

by RUTH I. JOHNSON

MOODY PRESS
CHICAGO

FOREWORD

This third volume of *Devotions for the Family Altar* is due to the popularity of the preceding two. It follows the same plan, giving suggestions for Bible reading, some practical applications of Bible truth, an interesting illustration—in all, a well-defined program for conducting daily devotions with children.

In his Foreword to *Devotions for the Family Altar No. 1*, Mr. Epp made two observations which are vital to this subject. One has to do with the very important principle of giving the Scriptures first place. He wrote, "These devotional lessons should not be used as substitutes for the Bible." The other is a suggestion on how to conduct devotions with children: "Each member of the family who is able to read should have his or her own Bible open at the place chosen for reading. Each should read a portion, and each should be given the opportunity to lead in prayer. If such a method is followed daily through the formative years, excellent habits which will endure for a lifetime will be established."

Ruth Johnson, who is a graduate of Moody Bible Institute, writes from an extensive background in children's and youth work. She is currently assistant editor of *Young Ambassador*, our monthly Gospel paper for youth. She is also the leader of the Ambassador Youth Choir heard each Sunday over the special network of the Back to the Bible Broadcast.

—John I. Paton
Literature Editor
Back to the Bible Publishers

CONTENTS

CHAPTER   PAGE

1. When God Talks 8
2. The Late Clock 10
3. Good or Bad Connections 12
4. The Pretty "No-Good" Cups 14
5. Going with Dad 16
6. The Clock That Worried 18
7. The Changing Leaves 20
8. Worship in Heathen Lands 22
9. The Mountain Climber's Fear 24
10. Not Safe to Wait 26
11. A Wheelbarrow Christian 28
12. Two Keys 30
13. Blackie or Tramp 32
14. The Lord's Supper 34
15. The Undelivered Message 36
16. The Pretender 38
17. The Covered Basket 40
18. A Pig in the House 42
19. The Good-for-Nothing Medicine 44
20. The Best Well 46
21. The Tough Coward 48
22. Ignored Warnings 50
23. God's Olympics 52
24. Spinach for the Missionary 54
25. Daddy Trims the Trees 56
26. A Little at a Time 58
27. Danny and the Water Puddle 60
28. God's Offering 62
29. The Quiet Family 64
30. A Soldier Comes Home 66

31. God's Shoes 68
32. Queen Victoria's Visit 70
33. Useless Umbrella 72
34. Black Houses 74
35. Pig and Cow Christians 76
36. Danny Gets Burned 78
37. God's Very Own Child 80
38. Danny's Bad Habit 82
39. The Teacher's Operation 84
40. The Plank and the Sawdust 86
41. The Empty Camera 88
42. God's Garden 90
43. A Gift for Brenda 92
44. Bimbo, the Second 94
45. Poison in the Jelly Jar 96
46. The Gum-ball Machine 98
47. A Fall into the Well 100
48. The Escaped Prisoner 102
49. Fudge and Chocolate Cake 104
50. Soldier with Disease 106
51. Too Far Away to Hear 108
52. Cleaning the Silver 110
53. "Chewing" the Bible 112
54. God Wanted Brother 114
55. The Planted Wristwatch 116
56. The Teacher's Sacrifice 118
57. A Brave Soldier 120
58. Not Too Young for Gifts 122
59. The Right Blood 124
60. Meeting the Governor 126

1

WHEN GOD TALKS

Songs: "I'll Be Somewhere Listening"; "Speak, My Lord"

Scripture: I Samuel 3:4-10

Story: Susan and Danny could not understand why they were sick. They had both been in bed for more than a week with a sore throat and cold.

"Why does God let us get sick?" asked Danny, who seemed to be grumbling more than his sister.

"Maybe He wants to teach you something," replied his mother.

"Why doesn't He teach me when I'm up? I can hear Him while I'm walking around."

"Can you?" Mother asked. There was a question in her voice that made Danny feel that she didn't agree with what he had said.

"Sometimes when we are playing, we forget to listen to God's voice. Sometimes when we are busy with this and that, God has to call several times before we take time to listen. But when we are sick in bed, we have nothing to distract us from the voice of God. You see, God speaks through His Word, and we stop and read His Word when we are down in bed."

Danny and Susan both listened to what Mother was saying. She was usually right, and they knew it.

"Do you remember the story of Samuel?" Mother continued. "Samuel was in bed. It was very quiet in the room. Then God called to him. He could have called during the daytime when Samuel was working around the temple, but He knew that everything would be quiet after Samuel was in bed, so He called then. Samuel's heart was quiet, and he listened to all that God had to tell him."

God often speaks to His children when they are sick or even at night when everything is quiet. He reminds them of Bible verses they have read, and teaches His lessons through these verses.

Memory Verse: "Speak, Lord; for thy servant heareth" (I Sam. 3:9).

Questions: 1. What was Danny grumbling about?
2. What did he ask his mother?
3. What was Mother's answer?
4. To whom did she compare Danny?
5. When did God call Samuel?
6. When does God often talk to us?

Prayer Requests: Pray for boys and girls who are sick. Pray that they will soon be well and strong. Pray also that they will listen to God when He talks to them while they are sick.

2

THE LATE CLOCK

Songs: "If Your Heart Keeps Right"; "A Heart Like Thine"

Scripture: Isaiah 1:16-20

Story: For the second day in a row, Danny had been late to school. "I can't understand why," he said to the teacher. "I thought I had plenty of time. I looked at our kitchen clock just before I left the house."

"Maybe you'd better check your clock," said the teacher. "It might be running slow."

That night, as Danny came home, he said, "Mother, is there anything wrong with our clock?"

Mother looked up at the clock on the kitchen wall. "Why, it must be running slow," she said. "The correct time must be about four o'clock, but the clock says it is only 3:45."

The next morning Daddy took the clock down to the jeweler and explained that Danny had been late to school two mornings.

"No wonder it's been running so slow," said the jeweler. "It's very dirty. It needs to be cleaned and adjusted."

them. He sees everything. All naughty things are sin.

Have you lied? Have you stolen or cheated? Have you disobeyed your parents? All of these things are wrong; they are sin, and they make very bad connections when we telephone to Heaven.

Before we can have good connections with God, we must put away all sinful things. Why not ask the Lord Jesus to make you clean and good and pure? Tell Him that you want good connections, so that you can talk with Him any time.

Memory Verse: "If I regard iniquity in my heart, the Lord will not hear me" (Ps. 66:18).

Questions: 1. What was Mother doing?
2. What happened on her long distance call?
3. What did the operator do?
4. What is our telephone to God?
5. What happens when there is sin in our lives?
6. How can we get good connections in our prayers to God?

Prayer Requests: Pray that your heart will be free from sin, so that you always have good connections with the Lord.

4

THE PRETTY "NO-GOOD" CUPS

Songs: "Jesus Bids Us Shine"; "I'm Gonna Work"

Scripture: Matthew 5:13-16

Story: Mother had a china cup collection. Daddy had bought them for her while he was in the army. Some of the cups had flowers, some had other designs, but every cup was beautiful.

"Why do you have that cup collection?" asked Susan, while she was watching Mother dust them one day.

"Just because I like them," said Mother. "Aren't they beautiful?" She picked up one of the cups and let Susan hold it. "Now, be careful with it, because it cannot be replaced." Susan quickly returned the cup to her mother, so she would not break it.

"Why don't we ever use them?" asked Danny, who was sitting at the couch on the other side of the room.

"Oh, I wouldn't let you use these cups," said Mother. "I'd be afraid you might break them."

"Well, they ain't no good on the buffet," said Danny.

"Aren't any good," corrected Susan.

Dad smiled as he looked up from his newspaper. "Well, either way, I think Danny's right. They're beautiful, but they aren't doing us much good."

Some Christians dress up beautifully on Sunday, but they just go to church and sit. They do not sing in the choir; they do not teach a Sunday school class; they do not help in the church; they do not even invite others to come to church. They are like the cups—pretty, but almost useless.

Memory Verse: "Let your light so shine before men, that they may see your good works, and glorify your Father which is in heaven" (Matt. 5:16).

Questions: 1. What was Mother's collection?
2. Where did she get them?
3. How were they being used?
4. Why didn't Mother want to use them?
5. How are these cups like some churchgoers?
6. How can you be a useful Christian?

Prayer Requests: Pray that you may be the kind of Christian who will let your light shine, so that others may see your good works and glorify the Lord Jesus.

5

GOING WITH DAD

Songs: "Anywhere with Jesus"; "Where He Leads Me"

Scripture: I Samuel 3:1-10

Story: Danny and his father were traveling on the train. Danny looked out of the window at the many things in the different cities. Danny liked to travel on trains. Sometimes he got to talk to the conductor, and once he even got to go to the front with the engineer.

"Do you remember the first time you rode on a train?" asked Daddy.

"Sure," answered Danny. "That was the day a man asked me where I was going."

"Yes, I'll never forget your answer," said Daddy. Danny had not forgotten it either. When the man had asked him where he was going, Danny had said, "I'm going wherever my dad goes."

Christian boys and girls ought to say that to the Lord Jesus. "I don't care where I go, Lord Jesus. I'll go anywhere You go."

Sometimes the Lord Jesus asks boys and girls to plan for missionary work in Africa; sometimes it is for India or South America. Sometimes He asks them to plan to go to the islands to preach the Gospel. We should never say, "No, Lord, I don't want to go there." We should say, as Danny said, "I don't care where I go. I'm just going with my dad." We should be very happy to go with our heavenly Father to tell others about the Lord Jesus.

Is God calling you today? Maybe you are too young to go now, but someday you will be older and then you should go wherever your heavenly Father leads you.

Memory Verse: "Go ye therefore, and teach all nations, baptizing them in the name of the Father, and of the Son, and of the Holy Ghost: Teaching them to observe all things whatsoever I have commanded you: and, lo, I am with you alway, even unto the end of the world" (Matt. 28:19,20).

Questions: 1. Where were Danny and his dad?
2. What happened on Danny's first train ride?
3. How should we answer the Lord's call?
4. Where does the Lord call some to go?
5. What should we never say to God?
6. What will you answer to God's call?

Prayer Requests: Pray that you will give your life fully to the Lord, and that you will be willing to go wherever He needs you.

6

THE CLOCK THAT WORRIED

Songs: "Why Worry When You Can Pray?"; "I Know Who Holds the Future"

Scripture: Luke 10:38-42

Story: Mother was reading a story to the children before they went to bed. It was about a big clock. Tick, tock, tick, tock—the pendulum on the clock was ticking back and forth, back and forth. Suddenly, the clock began to think of how many times he ticked every day. Then he figured out how many times he would have to tick during the year. Just thinking about this made the clock tired. Suddenly he decided to give up and stop working. It was just too much to expect a clock to tick that many times a year.

"I will not tick any more," he said.

Then he stopped. The room was quiet. The clock no longer worked.

After some time, the clock began to think about what he had decided. "Why should I worry about how many times I tick in a year," he said. "It's only one little tick at a time." So he decided to start again.

Danny and Susan liked the story and told their mother they would decide to follow Jesus and walk

18

with Him every day. They would not worry about what they were going to do when they grew up, for they belonged to Jesus.

Some people worry about all the things they need to do. But all of us should remember that we do not need to worry about the future, for it belongs to God. We need only to walk one step at a time when we have the Lord Jesus as our Saviour. He leads us and He tells us what to do. He tells us where to go.

We should do as the big clock did—decide not to worry about the future, but just take only one tick (step) at a time.

Memory Verse: "I will instruct thee and teach thee in the way which thou shalt go: I will guide thee with mine eye" (Ps. 32:8).

Questions: 1. What was Mother's story about?
2. What did the clock do all day long?
3. What did the clock finally decide to do?
4. Why did the clock decide this?
5. What should we do about our future?
6. Who will take care of our future?

Prayer Requests: Pray that you will learn to trust the Lord Jesus to lead you. Pray that you will not worry about the future, for to worry is sin.

7

THE CHANGING LEAVES

Songs: "The Beauty of Jesus"; "I Want To Be Like Jesus"

Scripture: Matthew 7:15-20

Story: Leaves on a tree often tell a story. Did you ever stand and look at a tree and its leaves? First, in the spring there are tiny buds. They do not seem to be very much, but after a little while they pop open and become beautiful leaves. These leaves give us shade. And all during the spring and summer they are beautiful and green. They are young and tender. Then in the fall, just before they drop to the ground, they begin to change color. The leaves become more beautifully colored then than at any other period in their lifetime. They are yellow, green, brown and red. The longer they hang on the tree the more beautiful they become.

Our lives should tell a story too. The longer we live for the Lord Jesus the more beautiful we should become, as Christians. Now, you are not very old. Maybe you are a new Christian, but you should be like the bright, beautiful green leaf just springing forth from a little bud on the tree. You can be very

"But what about yesterday?" asked one reporter. "You weren't afraid then."

"Oh, no!" said the mountain climber. "I did not think of myself. I thought of the man I had to rescue."

God gives Christian boys and girls, and men and women extra strength and courage when they need it. If you need to do something especially hard, ask God to give you strength. He will do it. You will be able to forget about yourself, and remember only the task you have in rescuing other people for the Lord Jesus.

Perhaps you think it is hard to go and tell someone about the Lord Jesus. Then go to Him and ask Him for special help. He will give it to you just at the very moment you need it.

Memory Verse: ". . . as thy days, so shall thy strength be" (Deut. 33:25).

Questions: 1. What did the mountain climber do?
2. Why did he do this?
3. Why was he able to do this?
4. What did the reporters want him to do the next day?
5. Why couldn't he do this?
6. From whom do we get our strength?

Prayer Requests: Pray that you may be strong in the Lord, and that you will have courage to obey Him.

10

NOT SAFE TO WAIT

Songs: "Tomorrow's Sun I May Not See"; "Come to Jesus Just Now"

Scripture: Psalm 95:7-11

Story: Susan and Danny's Uncle Ben was leaving town. Both Susan and Danny went with him to the train depot where he bought his ticket.

"There are two trains that you can take," said the ticket agent. "One leaves at ten o'clock and one leaves at twelve o'clock. Both trains will take you to the same place."

"If I take this twelve o'clock train," asked Uncle Ben, "can I make my connection all right?"

The ticket agent looked at him. "You only have seven minutes between trains," he replied.

"Well," repeated Uncle Ben, "is it safe to take that train?"

The ticket agent looked at Uncle Ben. "Sir," he said, "it is never safe to take the last chance."

Uncle Ben decided to take the early train so he would be sure to make his connection.

Almost everybody wants to go to Heaven. But some people say they should wait until they are older to prepare for Heaven. It is never safe to take the last chance. Maybe you will not live to be a grown man or a grown woman. Maybe you will die when you are still young.

It is not safe to wait, but it is safe to take the Lord Jesus as your Saviour today. Will you believe on Christ and ask Him to take away your sin? Ask Him to make your heart clean. Remember it is not safe to wait; you may not be alive tomorrow morning. Jesus is waiting for you to decide right now.

Memory Verse: "Jesus answered and said unto him, Verily, verily, I saw unto thee, Except a man be born again, he cannot see the kingdom of God" (John 3:3).

Questions: 1. Who was leaving town?
2. How many trains were there?
3. What did Uncle Ben ask the agent?
4. What did the agent reply?
5. What do some people think about Heaven?
6. Have you prepared for Heaven?

Prayer Requests: Pray that the Lord will help you so that you will not wait to accept Christ, even when the Devil whispers to you to wait.

11

A WHEELBARROW CHRISTIAN

Songs: "I'm Gonna' Work"; "In the Service of the King"

Scripture: Titus 2:11-15

Story: "Are you a 'wheelbarrow Christian'?" asked Danny's father.

Danny looked up from what he was doing. "Wheelbarrow Christian?" he asked. "What's that?"

Daddy did not answer. Instead he turned to Susan and asked, "Are you a 'wheelbarrow Christian'?"

"I don't know," Susan said. "Am I?"

Mother was sitting on the other side of the room, smiling. "I hope I'm not a 'wheelbarrow Christian,'" she said. She knew what Daddy meant.

"A 'wheelbarrow Christian,'" said Daddy, "is one who will go only as far as he is pushed."

Susan and Danny laughed, but they knew Daddy was trying to tell them something. Susan remembered the day she was not going to ask Mary to go to Sunday school with her, because it meant that Susan had to walk an extra block to get her friend. Daddy had made her go.

"I guess I am a 'wheelbarrow Christian,'" she confessed after thinking about it.

Danny remembered the time Mother asked him to take some clothes down to the church, so they could send them to the missionaries in Africa.

"I don't want to go all the way down there," Danny had complained, but Mother had told him he must go.

"I guess I'm a 'wheelbarrow Christian,'" he thought to himself.

Both Danny and Susan decided that day that they would never be "wheelbarrow Christians" again. From now on, they would look for things to do for the Lord Jesus and try to do them without being asked—especially without being pushed.

Memory Verse: "And whatsoever ye do, do it heartily, as to the Lord, and not unto men" (Col. 3:23).

Questions: 1. What did Daddy ask the twins?
2. What is a wheelbarrow Christian?
3. What did Susan remember?
4. What did Danny remember?
5. What did they decide?
6. Are you a wheelbarrow Christian?

Prayer Requests: Pray that you will realize how much the Lord has done for you and, in turn, give yourself ungrudgingly to His service.

12

TWO KEYS

Songs: "Search Me, O God"; "A Clean Heart"

Scripture: II Timothy 2:19-26

Story: Danny's father was holding two keys. One was very shiny, for Father had used it often. He kept putting it in and out of the lock, and this made it very shiny and clean. The other one had not been used at all. It had been lying in the garage where it had collected a lot of dirt and grease.

"Why is this one so dirty, and the other one so shiny?" asked Danny, pointing to the dirty key.

"This one is shiny," said Danny's father, "because it has been used. Dirt doesn't have time to settle in there. Every time I put it into the lock the dirt is pushed away."

Danny's father held up the other key. "This one," he said, "is dirty because it has never been used. Dust and grease have collected between the grooves. If I had used this key as often as I used the other one it would be clean too."

Sometimes Christian boys and girls do not use their lives for the Lord Jesus. There are many things they could be doing, but they are not busy in

God's work. They do not ask anyone to come to Sunday school and they do not pray for anyone. Often they are not even kind to their friends. They hardly ever read their Bibles, and they do not like to go to Child Evangelism class or Bible class. Sinful ways, just like dust and dirt and grease, begin to fill in the grooves and soon their lives are very dirty

We should be usable for the Lord Jesus. Just as the key slips into the lock and keeps clean while it is busy, so we should be busy, clean Christians for the Lord Jesus. What kind of Christian do you want to be? I hope you want to be a clean, good Christian.

Memory Verse: "Wash me thoroughly from mine iniquity, and cleanse me from my sin" (Ps. 51:2).

Questions: 1. How many keys did Danny's dad have?
2. What was the difference between the two keys?
3. Why was one so clean?
4. Why was the other one so dirty?
5. How do we become dirty Christians?
6. How can we keep clean?

Prayer Requests: Pray that your heart will not be cluttered and dirty with things of the world, but rather that you will be busy with the Lord's work.

13

BLACKIE OR TRAMP

Songs: "I Am Feeding on the Living Bread"; "With Eternity's Values in View"

Scripture: Acts 26:4, 9-16

Story: Blackie, Susan's dog, had a very bad habit. He ran around the neighborhood, dumped over the garbage cans, and ate the food he found there. Susan spanked him and tried everything to correct him. She even bought the very best dog food and placed it in his bowl, but Blackie just would not come home to eat.

"I'm going to change his name," said Susan. "From now on I'm going to call him 'Tramp.'"

"Why call him 'Tramp'?" asked Father who was sitting at the table.

"Because that's what he is," replied Susan. "He doesn't eat this real good dog food. He runs out to the neighbors' garbage cans and takes the scraps. That's just like a tramp."

"I guess he just doesn't realize what he's missing," said Mother. "He hasn't seen the difference between good dog food and bad garbage."

"I've tried to tell him," said Susan.

"But, honey," said Mother, "you must show him, not only tell him."

The next day Susan found her dog and led him down gently into the basement to the dog food. Blackie sniffed at it and then began to eat. In almost no time at all he had finished it.

"Look, Mother," said Susan, "he has eaten the dog food."

Each day Susan led Tramp downstairs to eat, and soon he did not run to the garbage cans any more.

"I guess I'll have to change his name again," said Susan. "He isn't a tramp any more."

The Lord Jesus has prepared a place in Heaven for us. It will have mansions and a golden street. We will live there forever, and ever, and ever. Everything will be wonderful. But in spite of all this some people do not seem to care. They live like Tramp did—around the garbage cans.

Memory Verse: "In my Father's house are many mansions: if it were not so, I would have told you. I go to prepare a place for you" (John 14:2).

Questions: 1. What was Blackie's bad habit?
2. How did Susan try to change him?
3. What new name did Susan give him?
4. What did Mother tell Susan to do?
5. What did Susan do about his name?
6. Have you prepared for Heaven?

Prayer Requests: Pray that you will love the Lord Jesus with all your heart and make ready for the home He has prepared for you.

14

THE LORD'S SUPPER

Songs: "In the Cross"; "Break Thou the Bread of Life"

Scripture: I Corinthians 11:23-29

Story: Susan and Danny sat very quietly in church. They watched as Mother and Daddy took part in the communion service. The service seemed very quiet and holy, and Susan and Danny felt quiet too.

"This do in remembrance of me," read the minister. Then everybody bowed quietly for prayer. Danny and Susan bowed too. It seemed that God was there. Everything was so quiet, so holy.

"What is communion?" asked Susan when they reached their home after the service.

"Communion is the same as the Lord's Supper," said Daddy. "Christians meet together at certain times to remember the Lord's death. And the Bible says that they are to keep on doing that until the Lord Jesus comes again."

"Is it for all Christians?" asked Danny.

"Yes," said Father. "The Bible says it is for those who believe; for those who have accepted Christ as their Saviour."

"Is it for me?" asked Susan.

For a long time Susan's father did not answer. Susan knew he was praying, for he was very quiet.

"It is if you are truly God's child," said Daddy.

"Daddy, I am a Christian," she said. "I accepted the Lord Jesus as my Saviour and I would love to remember His death with you and Mother."

"You must remember," said Daddy, "it is a very solemn time. When we think of how and why He died, our hearts are filled with sorrow at our sinfulness. At the same time we praise Him for dying for us."

Susan's face was very serious. "Daddy," she said, "since Jesus died for me, I want to remember Him at the communion service."

Daddy smiled. He knew that his little girl understood, and that when she began to take communion she would think seriously of the death of Jesus.

Memory Verse: "Behold the Lamb of God, which taketh away the sin of the world" (John 1:29).

Questions: 1. Where were Susan and Danny?
2. What were Mother and Daddy doing?
3. What did the minister read?
4. What did Susan ask her father?
5. Who should take communion?
6. What should Christians do during the communion service?

Prayer Requests: Ask God to help you to be very careful so you do not take communion if you have unconfessed sin in your heart.

15

THE UNDELIVERED MESSAGE

Songs: "Speed Away"; "Go Tell Someone About Jesus"

Scripture: I John 1:1-5

Story: "Susan," called Mother, putting down the telephone, "go and tell Mrs. Johns that Mr. Johns missed his train, so she shouldn't go to the station to meet him until later."

Susan had no thought of disobeying her mother, but she thought there was plenty of time to deliver the message later.

"May I have a piece of fudge?" she called as she walked through the kitchen.

"Yes, take one as you leave," said Mother.

Susan stood for a long time choosing her piece of fudge. Then she went outside, trying to remember what Mother had asked her to do. She could not remember. Instead of trying to find out, she began to play. After some time she remembered and ran to Mrs. Johns' house. She knocked on the back door, but nobody answered. Then she ran around to the front door, but there was still no answer.

"Mrs. Johns isn't there," Susan said on returning home.

"Did you just deliver the message now?" asked Mother.

"Yes," replied Susan. "I forgot about it until now."

"That message was urgent, Susan," said Mother. "Mrs. Johns will be greatly worried when her husband does not get off the train."

Susan was a poor messenger. Perhaps you are a poor messenger too. God has asked all of us to deliver the message of salvation. Have you failed to do so?

Memory Verse: "But if our gospel be hid, it is hid to them that are lost" (II Cor. 4:3).

Questions: 1. What did Mother ask Susan to do? 2. What did Susan do about the message? 3. What did she do when she remembered? 4. Where did Susan knock? 5. What did Mother tell Susan? 6. What kind of messenger are you?

Prayer Requests: Pray that you will not let one day slip by without telling someone about the Lord Jesus.

16

THE PRETENDER

Songs: "Do You Know That You've Been Born Again?"; "My Lord Is Real"

Scripture: Proverbs 6:16-23

Story: Susan's mother and father didn't have very much money, but it had never bothered Susan before. But now that Karen was in her class it seemed to make a difference. Karen's parents were very wealthy, and Karen had all the money she wanted.

"Are your folks rich?" Karen asked Susan one day.

Susan felt herself getting all hot and worried. "Oh, sure," she lied, "we've got lots of money!" She told Karen of all the toys, games, dolls and other things she had.

Susan felt guilty because she knew she was lying. She told herself she was only "pretending," so it surely couldn't be a real lie.

"I have more dresses than I can count," bragged Susan. Again she knew she was lying. But again she told herself that she was just "pretending."

The next day in school, Karen asked some of the other girls if Susan was really wealthy. The other girls laughed. "Oh, no, not Susan! Her folks don't have very much money," they said. "She must just be pretending."

Susan knew that this kind of pretending was lying, so she went to Karen and told her that she was sorry.

Some people pretend that they have Christianity. They go to church every Sunday. They try to act like Christians, but God knows that they are pretending. Before long they are "found out." Only those who have accepted the Lord Jesus as Saviour are really Christians.

Memory Verse: "This people draweth nigh unto me with their mouth, and honoreth me with their lips; but their heart is far from me" (Matt. 15:8).

Questions: 1. Who came to Susan's class?
2. What did Karen ask Susan?
3. What was Susan's answer?
4. What did Susan say about her dresses?
5. What did Susan realize about her pretending?
6. How do some people pretend?

Prayer Requests: Pray that God will give you grace and courage to fully surrender your heart to Christ so that you will be a real Christian and not a "pretending" Christian.

17

THE COVERED BASKET

Songs: "My Lord Knows the Way"; "Trust and Obey"

Scripture: Matthew 10:24-32

Story: Susan took the basket Mother had given to her and walked toward Aunt Nella's house. Mother had put something special in the basket, covered it carefully with a white cloth, and asked Susan to deliver it.

"Don't tip the basket," she said as Susan left the house.

As Susan walked down the street Danny met her.

"What's in the basket?" he asked.

"I don't know," said Susan.

"Well, why don't you look?" asked Danny.

Susan thought for just a moment. Then she said, "If Mother had wanted me to know, she would not have covered it and she would have told me."

Sometimes God does this to us. He hides things from our eyes. We do not need to know what will happen. That is up to God. He may tell us all about it sometime later, but we must learn to trust Him.

This is called, "living by faith." Christians should always live by faith.

Some people always seem to be asking, "What is this for, Lord? Why did you let this happen?" But we must learn to trust and obey the Lord, because we know that whatever the Lord does is good; it is perfect. He has a definite purpose for everything. His Word says: "All things work together for good to them that love God" (Rom. 8:28).

Have you learned to trust the Lord Jesus as your Saviour? Are you living by faith? Do you trust Him with everything in your life, even though it may mean sickness, or sadness, or other things?

He is God; learn to trust Him completely.

Memory Verse: "For we walk by faith, not by sight" (II Cor. 5:7).

Questions: 1. What did Mother ask Susan to do?
2. How was the basket fixed?
3. What did Danny ask?
4. What was Susan's answer?
5. What do some people ask God?
6. What should we learn to do?

Prayer Requests: Pray that you may learn to trust the Lord more completely and not question the things He sends into your life.

18

A PIG IN THE HOUSE

Songs: "Cleanse Me, O God"; "O, Be Careful"

Scripture: I John 1:5-10

Story: Mother was reading another story. This time it was about a pig. This pig made its way into the country home of some very wealthy people. The maid at the house had always kept everything clean and spotless. The furniture was always dusted, the floor was clean, and dishes were never left in the sink. She was a very good housekeeper.

One day the pig entered. He walked in through the basement door and walked into the kitchen. He found there was no one in the kitchen, so he rummaged around the table and the chairs, knocking them over on the floor. Then he went into the dining room and grunted and squealed. But before he could get into the living room, the lady who owned the house came home and spied him.

What do you think she did? Did she say, "Why, Mr. Pig, come right in. I'm so glad you came to visit us today"? Of course not! The woman not only called the maid, but she also clutched a broom in her hand,

and began to chase the pig out of the house. Then she went back into the house to repair the damage.

The pig is like our sins. Sometimes these sins get into our hearts and lives, and often they do much damage. Some people do not seem to care that these sins come into their lives. They let them stay there instead of chasing them out; or if they do chase them out, they do not clean up their lives from old sins.

We need to give ourselves to the Lord Jesus, and ask Him to help us chase these sinful habits out of our lives so that we will be good, clean houses for the Holy Spirit to live in.

Memory Verse: "Create in me a clean heart, O God; and renew a right spirit within me" (Ps. 51:10).

Questions: 1. Into what kind of home did the pig enter?
2. What did Mr. Pig do to the kitchen?
3. What happened when he went into the living room?
4. With what did the woman chase him out?
5. To what is the pig likened in our lives?
6. What should we do with sin?

Prayer Requests: Pray that you will recognize sins in your life and not let them stay there. Pray that you will confess any sin which is now in your heart.

19

THE GOOD-FOR-NOTHING MEDICINE

Songs: "Come to the Saviour"; "Him That Cometh unto Me"

Scripture: John 6:35-40

Story: Grandmother was sick and Mother had called the doctor. He wrote out a prescription and laid it on the table.

"Now send someone to the drugstore for these pills," he said, "and have Grandmother take them every three hours. I'm sure she will be feeling better very soon."

Mother sent Danny and Susan to the drugstore to get the medicine. In just a short time they were back with the box of pills.

"Oh," complained Grandmother as they entered her room, "I'm so sick."

"Here's your medicine," said Danny. "The doctor says this will make you feel better."

"Just put the box on the table," said Grandmother weakly.

After some time, Mother came back into the room and Grandmother seemed no better. "I can't understand why the medicine hasn't helped you," said

44

Mother. "Dr. Norton said it would. I'd better call him again."

"The medicine?" asked Grandmother. "Oh, I didn't take it!"

"But Dr. Norton told you to take it right away. It's good for you. In fact, it is the only thing that can help you."

"I'm sure it's good," said Grandmother. "I think it might even help me, but I just thought I'd wait for awhile. I just decided to put it off."

Some people talk that way about the Lord Jesus. They say, "Oh, church and God are fine but I'll wait until I'm ready to die, and then I will look to the Lord Jesus!"

How foolish! The Bible tells us that unless we accept God's way of salvation we will die. He has prepared the way of life—everlasting life. All we need to do is follow. Have you accepted Christ as your Saviour?

Memory Verse: "Almost thou persuadest me to be a Christian" (Acts 26:28).

Questions: 1. Who was sick?
2. What did the doctor give her?
3. Who went to get the medicine?
4. Why didn't it help Grandmother?
5. How are some people like that?
6. Who prepared salvation for us?

Prayer Requests: Pray that you will let the Lord Jesus come into your heart now to take away your sin, so that you will be made free from sin.

20

THE BEST WELL

Songs: "Jesus Gave Her Water"; "I Am Feeding on the Living Bread"

Scripture: John 4:7-15

Story: Danny and his father stood against the wall of a building watching the huge pumps from the fire engines try to drain the well. There were many fire trucks there pumping and pumping. They worked for a long time. After many, many hours, the men decided it would take too long to pump the well dry and gave up their work.

The Bible tells about another well, but this one could never be pumped dry. It is the well of everlasting life. The Lord Jesus is the Well of Life. No matter how many of us come to Him, we can always find a drink. He freely offers all the water of life. This well never runs dry, for He is the Son of God, the Lord Jesus. Have you taken this Water of Life?

One day a woman came to draw water from Jacob's well. Jesus had been on a long journey, so He stopped at this well to rest. When the woman came, Jesus talked to her. He said, "I am the well of life. I will give you everlasting life if you will just come to Me." After the woman talked to Jesus for awhile she believed on Him. Then she went and told other people about Jesus and they believed on Him too. Many people believed on Jesus that day because the woman believed on Jesus Christ, who is the Water of Life.

Have you received Jesus as your Saviour? If not, you should do so today. Jesus is God's Son. He will take your sin away and make you His child.

If you are a Christian, be sure to tell someone else about Jesus. The woman did this, and many people believed on Christ.

Memory Verse: "Blessed are they which do hunger and thirst after righteousness: for they shall be filled" (Matt. 5:6).

Questions: 1. What were the firemen trying to do?
2. What did they finally decide?
3. What kind of life does Jesus give?
4. When will this well run dry?
5. Who came to Jesus for water?
6. What did she do after she had seen Jesus?

Prayer Requests: Pray that you will see that you need Jesus to give you eternal life. If you have taken Jesus as your Saviour, pray for your friends who do not know Him.

21

THE TOUGH COWARD

Story: One of the tougher boys in school always Temptation"

Scripture: I Peter 5:6-11

Story: One of the tougher boys in school always wanted to fight. He made it a practice to pick a fight with a smaller boy almost every day. It was not long before the children in the neighborhood realized what the boy was doing.

"I've got an idea," said one of the smaller boys. "I am going to get my big brother, he's the same size as this other kid. Then when this tough kid comes to fight me, I'll just send my brother." Everyone agreed that this was a good idea.

The next time the tough boy started a fight, the smaller boy called his brother. Before long, the tough boy became frightened and ran away.

Christians, whether big or little, cannot fight Satan by themselves. He is as the tough boy. He picks on us because he knows we cannot fight him; but we know that he is afraid of Jesus.

We should say, as a little girl once said, "When Satan comes to my door to tempt me, I just send Jesus, and Satan gets scared and runs away."

The next time you are tempted to do something wrong, remember it is Satan who is tempting you. Why not ask Jesus to send him away? Satan is afraid of Jesus, because he knows that Jesus will fight and win all of our battles for us.

Memory Verse: "For whatsoever is born of God overcometh the world: and this is the victory that overcometh the world, even our faith" (I John 5:4).

Questions: 1. What did the tough boy do to the smaller boys?
2. What did one boy decide to do?
3. Who comes to "pick" on us?
4. What did a little girl say she would do?
5. Whom should we send?
6. Who will win our battles?

Prayer Requests: Pray that you may always remember to ask Jesus for help and not try to face Satan in your own strength.

22

IGNORED WARNINGS

Songs: "Say, Will You Be Ready?"; "Fire Song"

Scripture: Matthew 24:37-44

Story: Danny and Susan were visiting one of the large national parks with their mother and father. The guide continually warned them not to go near the bears. He even pointed to the signs that said, "Do not feed the bears."

All at once Danny heard an ambulance siren. He stepped out of the way, as he saw the ambulance come down the road in the national park.

"I think I know what happened," said the guide. "Somebody did not pay attention to the warnings."

"What do you mean?" asked Susan, who did not understand what the guide meant.

"I have warned you about the bears," said the guide. "I think someone probably did not heed the warning, and the bear jumped on him."

He was right. When they reached the place where the ambulance had stopped, they saw a little boy who had been attacked by a bear.

"I was just trying to feed him and pet him," said the boy, crying as they laid him on the stretcher.

"You see what I mean?" asked the guide. "He didn't obey the warnings."

God's Word has warnings too. One of them says that the wages of sin is death. But, like the little boy, many people refuse to listen to God's warning. Some day they will die. Then there will be everlasting death, because they did not obey God's warnings.

Memory Verse: "Therefore we ought to give the more earnest heed to the things which we have heard, lest at any time we should let them slip" (Heb. 2:1).

Questions: 1. Where were Danny and Susan?
2. Of what did the guide warn them?
3. What did they hear?
4. What had happened?
5. Why had this happened?
6. What is one of God's warnings?

Prayer Requests: Pray that you will take God's warnings seriously, and obey them and take Jesus as your Saviour before it is too late.

23

GOD'S OLYMPICS

Songs: "Toe the Mark, Get Set"; "V Is for Victory"

Scripture: I Corinthians 9:24-27

Story: "Get ready. Get set. Go!" cried the starter, and the two boys ran. Dick was sure he was going to win the race because he had won last year's race. But in just a few minutes Jerry passed him and became the winner. Dick was angry with Jerry and with everyone else, because he had lost.

Dick's teacher reminded him that Jerry had spent hours and days preparing for the race, and Dick had not stayed after school one day to practice.

Men who run in the Olympic races are not chosen hastily. No. They usually begin their preparation and training while they are very young. They keep in training day after day and week after week. Each year they find that they become stronger and faster.

Each day they are careful to get the right kind of food and at night they try to get the right amount of rest. This helps build their bodies. They refuse anything that would harm their bodies.

No doubt their careers started as they became the fastest runners in their neighborhood, then the best runners in the school, the city, the state, and finally in the country.

We too should prepare for the Christian race. We should begin every morning by eating (reading) from the Word of God, and spending time in prayer. This will strengthen us spiritually and make us strong for the Lord Jesus.

If we want to be in one of "God's Olympics," we must be willing to prepare and sacrifice so that we too may become winners.

Memory Verse: "I press toward the mark for the prize of the high calling of God in Christ Jesus" (Phil. 3:14).

Questions: 1. Who won the race?
2. Why did Dick lose?
3. How do the Olympic runners train?
4. How did they become Olympic runners?
5. What kind of race do we have?
6. How can we prepare for this race?

Prayer Requests: Pray that as you read God's Word each day, you will grow stronger in Him and run the Christian race well.

24

SPINACH FOR THE MISSIONARY

Songs: "Ready Am I"; "I'm Going Forth"

Scripture: Acts 9:10-16

Story: "I'm going to be a missionary when I grow up," Danny said to his father at the dinner table.

"Do you think you can be a good missionary?" asked Danny's dad.

"Sure. I'll be able to do lots of things. After I finish school here, I'll go to a Bible school and college. Then I'll learn to do some special things, and soon I'll go to Africa and be a missionary. I want to tell all those people about Jesus."

"Well, that's fine," said Daddy, "but there are some other things you need to learn." He passed the dish of spinach to Danny.

"I hate spinach," said Danny. "I don't want any."

Daddy seemed to ignore what he said, and put a spoonful of spinach on Danny's plate. Mother poured him a glass of milk.

"I don't want any milk, Mother," said Danny. "I don't like milk."

"Son," said Daddy, "are you sure you can be a missionary?"

"Sure, I'm sure. I told the Lord Jesus I'd do anything."

"Would you even eat spinach?"

"Spinach!" said Danny. "What's that got to do with being a missionary?"

"Or drink your milk?" added Mother.

Daddy explained to him that a missionary had to be willing to do many things. "You can't be finicky and fussy," he said. "You have to learn to eat all kinds of food, sleep in all kinds of places and be thankful and content while you are doing it."

Danny realized he would not be a very good missionary unless he learned to do these things. So he determined in his heart that he would be a good missionary, even if it meant he had to learn to eat spinach.

Memory Verse: "And he said to them all, If any man will come after me, let him deny himself, and take up his cross daily, and follow me" (Luke 9:23).

Questions: 1. What did Danny want to be?
2. Where did he want to go?
3. What did Daddy pass to him?
4. What was Danny's answer?
5. What did Daddy say about missionaries?
6. What did Danny determine to do?

Prayer Requests: Pray that you will gladly give yourself to the Lord Jesus when He shows you His plan for your life.

25

DADDY TRIMS THE TREES

Songs: "Nothing but Leaves"; "Have I Done My Best for Jesus?"

Scripture: John 15:1-8

Story: Danny's father was trimming the trees out in the back yard. "You're sure spoiling these trees," said Danny.

"It does look that way, doesn't it?" replied Daddy as he continued to cut another branch from the tree. "Well, I guess that's it," he said, and walked over to where Danny was standing.

"You forgot this tree," said Danny.

"No, I did not forget it," replied Daddy. "I am leaving this one to teach you a lesson."

"A lesson?" Danny asked. "What kind of lesson?"

"As I was trimming these trees you thought I was spoiling them. Next summer I want to show you what happens to one you do not trim. These that I pruned will have more fruit. The one I did not trim will not bear much fruit. You just wait and see."

It was true. The next summer when the fruit began to come out on the trees, there was only one tree that did not have very much. It was the tree that Daddy had not trimmed.

Sometimes we think "trimming" hurts, but the Lord Jesus permits it in our lives in order to make us better Christians. Like the trees, we are to bear fruit; but if we do not let Christ prune us, our fruit will not be as plentiful.

Trimming or pruning hurts, but only for a short time, and then we become more beautiful trees, bringing forth much fruit for Christ.

Memory Verse: "But he knoweth the way that I take: when he hath tried me, I shall come forth as gold" (Job 23:10).

Questions: 1. What was Daddy doing to the trees?
2. What did Danny think he was doing?
3. Why did Daddy leave one tree?
4. What happened to those that were pruned?
5. How are we like trees?
6. What happens to Christians who are trimmed?

Prayer Requests: Pray that you will be willing to let God take anything out of your life that is hindering Him from working through you.

26

A LITTLE AT A TIME

Songs: "Search the Scriptures Daily"; "Thy Word Have I Hid in My Heart"

Scripture: Psalm 119:9-15

Story: "I can't learn these verses," complained Susan. "I have tried and tried, but I just can't do it."

Mother looked up from the dishes she was washing. "What do you mean?" she asked.

"These Bible verses," grumbled Susan. "We are supposed to learn 100 of them or we can't go to camp."

"Why, that shouldn't be so hard," said Mother. "But I think you are doing it the wrong way."

"What do you mean?"

"Let me tell you a story," said Mother. "Once there was a painter who had a very difficult picture to paint. At first it worried him. How would he ever get this wonderful picture done? Each day he thought and worried about it. He decided that he would never get it done. Then he had an idea. Every day he set aside a certain amount of time to paint. He never let anything take the place of that time when he was to paint. Every day at the regular time he would work. Before long he had the entire picture done.

"I think if you will take a certain time each to memorize God's Word, one verse at a time, even one line at a time, you will soon have your verses learned."

Susan took her mother's suggestion and spent a certain time every day learning her verses and reviewing some of the others. By the time summer came and camp was ready, Susan knew more than her 100 verses. In Sunday school the teacher commended her for learning so many.

Memory Verse: "I will delight myself in thy statutes: "I will not forget thy word" (Ps. 119:16).

Questions: 1. Why was Susan grumbling?
2. How many verses was she to learn?
3. What was the reward for this?
4. What did Mother tell her?
5. How did the painter get his picture done?
6. How did Susan learn her verses?

Prayer Requests: Pray that you will take time to learn God's Word so that you will hide it in your heart.

27

DANNY AND THE WATER PUDDLE

Songs: "I'll Be True, Lord Jesus"; "Dare to Be a Daniel"

Scripture: Ephesians 6:10-18

Story: Danny was wearing his Sunday shoes and his best suit to school. There was going to be a party, and everyone was to dress up.

"You'd better wear your rubbers," said Mother, "for it rained last night, and I don't want you to get your new shoes dirty."

"Mother," said Danny, "if I promise not to walk in any water, may I go to school without my rubbers?"

Mother agreed, and Danny left for school.

All the way to school Danny watched every step he took. He carefully avoided all the water puddles on the sidewalks and on the street.

On the way home Danny walked with an older boy. "Let's splash the next puddle," said the boy.

"Oh, no," said Danny, "I've got my new shoes on! I can't!"

"A little water won't hurt them," said the boy.

"But I promised my mother," said Danny.

"You're a sissy," replied the boy. "You're just afraid. You're chicken."

"I am not," he answered, "and to prove it I'll splash the next puddle."

A few minutes later Danny reached home. His shoes were wet and there was mud on his clothes.

"I didn't want to be called 'chicken,' so I did what he told me to do," he confessed.

Some boys and girls will do what someone else tells them to do even if it means disobeying their parents. This is wrong.

Danny was punished for his disobedience. We too will suffer when we disobey God and do things that are not pleasing to the Lord Jesus.

Memory Verse: "Watch ye, stand fast in the faith, quit you like men, be strong" (I Cor. 16:13).

Questions: 1. Why was Danny dressed up?
2. What did he promise his mother?
3. What did the older boy ask Danny to do?
4. What did he call Danny?
5. How did Danny explain it to his mother?
6. What happens when we disobey God?

Prayer Requests: Pray that you will have courage to say "no" whenever you are tempted to sin.

28

GOD'S OFFERING

Songs: "Give of Your Best to the Master"; "What Shall I Give Thee, Master?"

Scripture: I Corinthians 16:1,2; II Corinthians 9:6,7

Story: Susan and Danny had been wondering whether or not they should tithe their money. Daddy had explained to them that part of their money really belonged to God, but they weren't sure which part or how much. That day after they came home from Sunday school, Danny said, "I gave a nickel in the offering today."

"I gave a dime," said Susan. "Next Sunday I'm going to give a quarter."

"I think I might give a dollar," boasted Danny.

"What makes you say that?" asked Daddy.

"We heard a swell story today," said Susan. "It was about a man who gave his very last dollar to the Lord; he didn't even have enough money for food. But the next morning in the mail he got a letter with a ten-dollar bill in it. God rewarded him for giving everything he had."

"So we decided to give a lot of money next Sunday," said Danny, "to see if God would give us ten times more."

For a moment their father looked at them. Then he shook his head. "That isn't why you give money to God," he said. "You don't give it to get it back. That's selfishness. You give it because of your love for Him. Would you be willing to give that dollar if you thought you wouldn't get a cent back?"

There was a long silence. "I guess I would," said Susan finally.

"I guess I would too," agreed Danny.

When we give grudgingly to God it is not real giving. True giving never looks for anything in return. When we give it, it should be done cheerfully and with much love.

Memory Verse: "Freely ye have received, freely give" (Matt. 10:8).

Questions: 1. How much did Susan give in the offering?
2. What did Danny plan to give the next Sunday?
3. Why did they want to give this amount?
4. What did the man get from God?
5. Why should we give to God?
6. How should we give to God?

Prayer Requests: Pray that you will give your life, your talents, and your money to God because you love Him.

29

THE QUIET FAMILY

Songs: "Did You Think to Pray?"; "Keep on Praying"

Scripture: Daniel 6:10-13

Story: "I wish we didn't have to have family prayers every night," grumbled Susan. "I think it would be enough just to do it on Sunday nights."

Mother and Daddy looked at each other. "Is that all right with everyone?" asked Daddy.

"Sure," said Danny. Mother did not answer for she knew that Daddy had an idea up his sleeve.

"All right," he said. "No family prayers until next Sunday. And by the way, we won't talk to each other here at home between now and Sunday either."

"Why?" questioned Danny. "Why can't we talk to each other?"

Daddy acted as though he hadn't heard the question.

All that day everything was quiet in the house. Susan and Danny wanted to ask what was going on, but somehow they thought they shouldn't.

The next morning when Susan got up she ran downstairs, put her arms around her mother and was all ready to say, "Good morning," when she remembered.

Danny came down too. "I don't like our house like this," he shouted. "I want to talk."

Daddy followed the children into the kitchen. "Well," he said, "I just wanted you to know how God must feel when nobody talks to Him except on Sunday."

Some boys and girls think prayer time is for Sunday only. But since prayer time is a time for all God's children to talk with Him, and to let Him talk with them, it should be held every day. Have you talked with Him today?

Memory Verse: "Evening, and morning, and at noon, will I pray, and cry aloud: and he shall hear my voice" (Ps. 55:17).

Questions: 1. What did Susan want?
2. What did Daddy say to that?
3. What did he say about the family?
4. What happened when Daddy came downstairs?
5. How did Daddy explain it?
6. What did they learn from this?

Prayer Requests: Pray that your heart will always be in touch with God, and that you will take special time each day to be alone with Him in prayer.

30

A SOLDIER COMES HOME

Songs: "He's Coming Back Again"; "Lord, Keep Me Shining for Thee"

Scripture: Matthew 25:1-13

Story: Mr. and Mrs. Matthews lived next door to Susan and Danny. Their oldest son was in the army. Every day they looked for him to come home. "I'll be home on furlough in just a few days," his telegram had said.

Every night Mr. and Mrs. Matthews left a light in the window. Even in the middle of the night, when everything else was dark, this lamp continued to shine. Finally their boy came home. As he walked up the street, he saw the little light in the window.

Mr. and Mrs. Matthews had been waiting for their son. They expected him and looked for him every day. They were prepared for his coming.

The Lord Jesus tells us in His Word that He is coming. He said, "I will come again." Christian people are ready for Christ's return. They are looking for Him, just as Mr. and Mrs. Matthews looked for their son. But some people do not seem to care about the Lord's coming. When Jesus comes they will be left behind, for they will not be ready for Him. Unless people are saved when Jesus comes they will be left behind.

Jesus warned us to be ready, for He is coming at a time when the world will not expect Him.

If Jesus should come today, would you be ready to go with Him? The only way to be ready is to accept Him as your Saviour. But you must do it now before it is too late, then when He comes you will be one of those whom He will take with Him.

Memory Verse: "And if I go and prepare a place for you, I will come again, and receive you unto myself; that where I am, there ye may be also" (John 14:3).

Questions: 1. Who lived next door to Susan and Danny?
2. For whom were they waiting?
3. What did they do to show they were expecting him?
4. Who is coming again?
5. Who will be left behind?
6. How can we be ready when Jesus comes?

Prayer Requests: Pray that you will be watching for the Lord Jesus to come back and that you will have your lights shining for Him.

31

GOD'S SHOES

Songs: "Walking with Jesus"; "I'll Go Where You Want Me to Go"

Scripture: Luke 10:1-9

Story: Clump! Clump! Clump! Danny came walking down the steps in his father's shoes.

"Look, Dad," he said, "I'm wearing your shoes."

"Aren't they a little big?" asked Danny's father.

"Sure, but I'm wearing my shoes inside of yours," said Danny.

That night, as the family sat down to dinner, Daddy took the devotional book and began reading. "God has some shoes," read Daddy, "but He needs somebody to wear them. Sometimes God's shoes go to Africa; sometimes they only go to Sunday school here in America, but God needs somebody to wear His shoes. I wonder who it will be?"

As Daddy put down the book, Danny asked, "What does that mean?"

Then Daddy explained. "Whatever we do, we must do for the Lord Jesus. We can step into God's shoes just as you stepped into my shoes, Danny."

Do you want to be God's missionary? Step into God's shoes and go to the country where He leads. Do you want to be a good witness in school? Step into God's shoes, for He is going to school and He needs somebody to be His witness there.

Are you ready to be one of God's helpers? Step into His shoes and say, "I'll go where you want me to go, dear Lord."

Memory Verse: "Now then we are ambassadors for Christ" (II Cor. 5:20).

Questions: 1. What was Danny wearing?
2. What did Danny do to make the shoes fit?
3. What did Daddy read about that night?
4. Where are some places that God's shoes are going?
5. What does God need?
6. What should all Christians say to the Lord?

Prayer Requests: Pray that you will be one of God's messengers and be a willing worker wherever He leads you.

32

QUEEN VICTORIA'S VISIT

Songs: "Jesus Is All the World to Me"; "Christ Liveth in Me"

Scripture: Joshua 24:14-24

Story: Many, many years ago, Queen Victoria decided to visit a poor little widow in her very humble cottage. The widow was a very fine Christian woman. She loved the Lord Jesus and talked about Him a great deal. The day after Queen Victoria had visited her, the neighbors came in to see her.

"Granny," they said, "who is the most honored guest you have ever had in your home?" Because she was such a fine Christian, they were sure she would say Christ. But old Granny surprised them.

"Why, Her Majesty, the Queen," said Granny.

This time the neighbors thought they had "caught" Granny. "So she wasn't really thinking about Jesus," they said. Finally one of the men spoke up.

"You mean to tell me that you think more of having had Queen Victoria in your house than the Lord Jesus? I thought you believed in Jesus and loved Him."

"Oh," said Granny with a smile, "you said a guest! Jesus is not a guest in my house. He lives here."

The neighbors did not have any more to say, for they knew that Granny loved the Lord Jesus so much that she treated Him as one of the members of her family. He never left. He belonged in her house.

Does the Lord Jesus live in your house? Does He live there all the time, or can He just come in as a guest on certain days, maybe Sunday? Do you treat Him as someone who just comes and goes, or does He really live in your heart?

Memory Verse: "I am crucified with Christ: nevertheless I live; yet not I, but Christ liveth in me" (Gal. 2:20).

Questions: 1. Who visited the widow?
2. What kind of woman was this widow?
3. What did the neighbors ask her?
4. What was her answer?
5. What did she say about Jesus?
6. Is Jesus a guest at your house, or does He live there?

Prayer Requests: Pray that you may treat Christ as One who is with you constantly and not just a guest.

33

USELESS UMBRELLA

Songs: "Let the Book Live to Me, O Lord"; "I Love to Tell the Story"

Scripture: II Kings 22:8-13

Story: Danny and Susan laughed as they listened to the story Mother was reading to them. An elderly man was walking in the rain. A storekeeper saw him and came to the door. "Say, there," he called, "step up here, and I'll give you an umbrella." The elderly man took the umbrella and walked out of the store. The storekeeper watched him for awhile, but the man did not open the umbrella. Instead he put it under his coat and continued to walk in the rain. Soon he met another man on the street.

"Why don't you use your umbrella?" asked the man.

The elderly man looked at his friend. "Why, the storekeeper was so nice to loan it to me. I cannot get it wet for him."

We think this elderly man was very foolish, because he did not make use of the umbrella and it did him no good. The storekeeper had given it to the man to keep him from getting wet, but the elderly man had not used it.

Sometimes boys and girls do this with God's Word, especially if they have a new Bible. They leave it on the dresser or the table. They dust it off, and keep it "just so," but they never use it. God did not intend for us just to have a beautiful Bible on a table. He said that we should hide His Word in our hearts. If we do not memorize God's Word, if we do not read from the Bible, we are just like the foolish man who hid the umbrella under his coat, so that it would not get wet.

Memory Verse: "Be ye doers of the word, and not hearers only" (James 1:22).

Questions: 1. What did the storekeeper give the man?
2. What did the elderly man do with it?
3. Why didn't he use it?
4. What do some people do with their Bibles?
5. What are we to do with God's Word?
6. Whom are we like if we do not use it?

Prayer Requests: Pray that you will read your Bible so that you can live according to the Scriptures and be a good witness to others.

34

BLACK HOUSES

Songs: "My Heart Was Black with Sin"; Whiter Than the Snow"

Scripture: Matthew 23:25-28

Story: Susan and Danny were traveling on the train with their parents. They were going to visit their grandmother. The train tracks were very near some of the houses. Danny and Susan thought they had never seen so many shabby places. As they passed through one city, they noticed that almost all of the houses were painted dark. Many of them were even painted black.

"Why would anyone paint his house black?" asked Danny.

Susan acted as though she knew all the answers. "Why, so it won't get dirty."

Mother had heard their conversation and thought she could help her children. "It still gets dirty, Susan," she said. "It's just that it doesn't show as much. But the dirt is still there."

Both Danny and Susan were quiet. Mother had often talked to them about sin. "Sometimes other people can't see our sin," she had said, "but it is still there."

If Danny and Susan had gone up to the house and touched it, they would have become dirty. God knows that our lives are dirty too. They are full of sin, even though we often try to cover them up with good works.

Just because the people had painted their houses black did not mean that they were not dirty. The black paint was only a "cover up."

Memory Verse: "The Lord seeth not as man seeth; for man looketh on the outward appearance, but the Lord looketh on the heart" (I Sam. 16:7).

Questions: 1. Where were Danny and Susan going?
2. What did they see in one city?
3. Why did Susan say the houses were painted black?
4. What did their mother say about it?
5. What do some people try to do with sin?
6. What was the black paint used for?

Prayer Requests: Pray that you will not "pretend" to be a Christian, but that Christ may really be your Saviour.

35

PIG AND COW CHRISTIANS

Songs: "What Shall I Give Thee, Master?"; "If I Had a Thousand Lives to Live"

Scripture: Luke 6:30-38

Story: Everybody in church laughed as the minister was telling a story. But they listened carefully. "A rich man came to a preacher one day and said, 'Why is it everybody criticizes me for being miserly? Don't they know that I have made out a will, and when I die everything will go to the church?'

"The preacher seemed to change the subject. 'Let me tell you about the pig and the cow,' he said. 'One day a pig went to a cow and said, "Why is it I am so unpopular? People always talk about you as being kind and gentle. But you only give milk and cream. I give more than that. I give bacon and ham, but nobody seems to like me. Why is it?"

" 'The cow thought for a minute, then she said, "Well, maybe it is because I give mine while I am still living. You don't give yours until you are dead.' "

Sometimes boys and girls and big people too are like the pig. They do not give their money to God, they just save it for themselves. They say, "I will give it all to God when I die." But they forget that God needs money to do His work now while they are living.

We should be willing to work for Jesus today. We should not tell Him that we will do it later. We are never sure that we will have another day.

Are you a pig Christian or a cow Christian? I am sure you are one or the other.

Memory Verse: "He which soweth sparingly shall reap also sparingly; and he which soweth bountifully shall reap also bountifully" (II Cor. 9:6).

Questions: 1. Who came to the preacher?
2. What did the preacher seem to do?
3. What did the pig say to the cow?
4. What was the cow's answer?
5. What do some people do about their money?
6. Are you a pig Christian or a cow Christian?

Prayer Requests: Pray that you will be a cheerful giver, not only of your possessions, but also of yourself.

36

DANNY GETS BURNED

Songs: "O, Be Careful"; "True-hearted, Whole-hearted"

Scripture: Philippians 4:4-9

Story: Danny was visiting his grandmother on the farm. He went to see her every chance he had. Whenever he went there his appetite seemed to get bigger and bigger. He told Grandmother he thought he could eat all day.

One day he tried it. He ate and ate, and before long he was not feeling too well. He went into the house and sat down on the floor by the open fire.

"You have to be careful," said Grandmother, "that you don't get too close to the fire. It can really burn."

Danny liked the feeling of the heat. It was so nice and warm. Soon he found himself moving closer and closer to it. All at once he realized there was a big brown spot on the knee of his pants. As he fingered it, it became a hole.

"Look," he said to his grandmother. "Look at this brown spot."

"Yes," said Grandmother, "I warned you not to go too near the fire, because while it gives heat to the room, it also burns."

There are several things that are good if done moderately, but when they are overdone they are wrong. Eating is good, but overeating as Danny did is sin. Playing is good, but all play is not good.

The fire was good too. It gave heat to the room. But it could also burn, and Danny found that out.

We should be "temperate" in all things. That means that we should not overdo in anything, but that we should live moderately as God intended for us to live.

Memory Verse: "Let your moderation be known unto all men. The Lord is at hand" (Phil. 4:5).

Questions: 1. Where was Danny visiting?
2. What did he like to do there?
3. What happened when he ate too much?
4. What happened when he got too close to the fire?
5. What did you learn about eating and playing?
6. What two things can fire do?

Prayer Requests: Pray that God will help you "prove all things." Pray that you will be willing to choose to do the things that are acceptable to Him.

37

GOD'S VERY OWN CHILD

Songs: "A Child of the King"; "Now I Belong to Jesus"

Scripture: Galatians 4:3-7

Story: "Am I adopted?" asked Danny at the dinner table one evening.

Daddy laughed. "No, son. You look too much like me for that. You were born into our family."

"What does adopted mean?" asked Susan, who was listening carefully to the conversation.

"You know Mike Anderson, who lives next door?" asked Mother. "He was adopted. His mother and father did not have any children, so they went to the orphanage one day, and said, 'We want the nicest little boy you have.' And the orphanage gave them Mike."

"Is he their very own?" asked Susan.

"Yes," continued Mother. "Mr. and Mrs. Anderson legally adopted Mike. They have papers to prove he belongs to them and they even gave him their name. No one can take him away. He is their son."

"I have a paper that shows I belong to Someone

too," said Daddy. Then he took his Bible and read, "Now are ye the sons of God."

"Can I be God's son?" asked Danny.

"Yes," replied his father, "you can if you will accept Christ and become His child."

"How can I accept Him?" asked Danny.

"Just by telling Him that you have sinned, and that you want Him for your Saviour. You have sinned, haven't you?" asked Mother.

"Oh, sure, lots of times!" confessed Danny.

"Then just tell Jesus that you are a sinner, and ask Him to make you clean and good and pure. Ask Him to make you His very own child."

That day Danny became God's very own child.

Memory Verse: "But as many as received him, to them gave he power to become the sons of God, even to them that believe on his name" (John 1:12).

Questions: 1. What did Danny ask his parents?
2. What was his father's answer?
3. Who in the neighborhood was adopted?
4. What did the Andersons give to Mike?
5. What did Daddy say about belonging?
6. How can you become God's very own child?

Prayer Requests: Pray that God will take away your sin and make you His very own child.

38

DANNY'S BAD HABIT

Songs: "Oh, Be Careful"; "Angry Words"

Scripture: Luke 6:36,37; Matthew 18:21,22

Story: Danny had a very bad habit of making a clucking sound from the corner of his mouth. It annoyed Susan. Every time he did it Susan shouted irritably, "Stop it." Before long, Danny realized that he could irritate his sister by continuing to do it. So whenever she called it to his attention he would insist on doing it over and over again. Often it ended in a very bad quarrel.

Who was wrong? Danny, for not taking his sister's suggestion and trying to break the bad habit when he knew it bothered her? Or Susan, for becoming irritable and not being kind when her brother did it and often forgot?

The children took it to their mother. "Both of you are very wrong," she said. "Danny, if you have a habit that irritates your sister, you should try to break that habit. You should thank her when she calls it to your attention."

"But she just screams at me," said Danny.

"Yes, I've noticed that, Susan," said Mother, "and that is where you are wrong. You should be patient with your brother and try to help him overcome his bad habit. You should not become irritable and angry with him. Danny, by all means you should not continue to do that which you know bothers your sister. And Susan, you are wrong too in shouting at Danny and becoming angry with him."

Sometimes we try to put the blame on the other person, but often it is our fault too. We are permitting sin to control our lives whether we are the ones with the bad habits, or the ones who become angry and irritable. Both of these are sin. Both of them need to be overcome before we can be good Christians.

Memory Verse: "Confess your faults one to another, and pray one for another, that ye may be healed" (James 5:16).

Questions: 1. What was Danny's bad habit?
2. What did it do to Susan?
3. What did Danny do when he knew it annoyed her?
4. According to Mother, which one was wrong?
5. What do we often try to do?
6. What should we do when sin controls our lives?

Prayer Requests: Pray that the Lord will give you a loving, kind, and forgiving spirit toward others.

39

THE TEACHER'S OPERATION

Songs: "This One Thing I Know"; "Only a Touch of Thy Hand, Dear Lord"

Scripture: John 9:1-7

Story: Danny and Susan had a substitute teacher in school. Their regular teacher was in the hospital. She had to have an operation on her eyes. The substitute teacher explained to the class that it would be several weeks before their regular teacher would be back.

Each evening Danny and Susan remembered their teacher in prayer. They asked the Lord Jesus to take care of her and help her so that she would be able to see very soon. Almost every day they would ask their mother to call the hospital or the doctor to see how their teacher was. After many days the doctor said, "The operation is successful. Your teacher will be able to see."

One day a blind man came to Jesus. He said, "Jesus, please help me to see. Take my blindness away." Jesus stooped to the ground and made some clay and put it on the blind man's eyes.

"Now, go wash in the pool," said Jesus. The blind man obeyed. As soon as he washed, he could see. Jesus had healed him immediately.

It did not take days and days for this blind man to get his sight, as it did Danny's and Susan's school teacher. When Jesus does something He does it right away.

Many people are blind, but they do not know it. They are spiritually blind. That means that they are sinners and have not asked Jesus to take their sin away. Are you spiritually blind, or have you accepted Christ as your Saviour? He will take your sin away the moment you ask Him.

Memory Verse: "The Lord openeth the eyes of the blind" (Ps. 146:8).

Questions: 1. Why did the children have a substitute teacher?
2. What did Susan and Danny do each evening?
3. With whom did Mother check every day?
4. What did Jesus do for the blind man?
5. How are some people blind?
6. When will Christ take our sin away?

Prayer Requests: Pray that the Lord Jesus will open your eyes to see Him, and that you will open your heart to receive His wonderful salvation.

40

THE PLANK AND THE SAWDUST

Songs: "Have I Given Jesus My Heart?"; "Every Moment of Every Day"

Scripture: Luke 6:40-45

Story: Danny's father was sawing a big piece of wood. The sawdust was falling to the basement floor. Danny ran his fingers through the sawdust.

"Did you know that the Bible talks about a plank and sawdust?" asked Danny's father.

Danny looked up in question at his dad. He could not remember any verse that said anything about sawdust or a big piece of wood.

"You run upstairs and get my Bible," continued Danny's father, "and I'll show you."

Danny ran up the stairs, two at a time, and returned with his father's Bible.

"Here's the verse," Daddy said, leafing through the pages of his Bible. "It uses some different words, but it means exactly the same thing." Then he read, "And why beholdest thou the mote that is in thy brother's eye, but considerest not the beam that is in thine own eye?"

Daddy closed the Bible and put it down on the basement step. "Another translation explains it this way, 'Why do you see the speck that is in your brother's eye, but do not notice the log that is in your own eye?'" Danny was beginning to understand what the verse meant.

"It is very easy," continued Daddy, "to see the faults in somebody else. But sometimes we forget that we have faults too. It is like this plank of wood and the sawdust. The other person's faults should become just like sawdust or a tiny speck compared to this big plank, or the log, in our own lives."

From then on every time Danny saw a big piece of wood or some sawdust he thought of the Bible lesson that his daddy had taught him. He was not to find fault with other people, but to ask Jesus to take the sin out of his own life first.

Memory Verse: "Judge not, that ye be not judged" (Matt. 7:1).

Questions: 1. What was Daddy doing?
2. What did he ask Danny to get?
3. What did he say was in the Bible?
4. What does that verse mean?
5. What should we do when we see other people's faults?
6. What should we do about our own faults?

Prayer Requests: Ask the Lord to keep you from finding fault with others, and to help you to pray for them. Thank Him for forgiving all your sins.

41

THE EMPTY CAMERA

Songs: "Into My Heart"; "My Lord Is Real"

Scripture: Matthew 7:15-23

Story: Grandmother and Grandfather were visiting at Danny's and Susan's house. They lived more than a thousand miles away, so they could not come to visit very often.

"We want to be sure and take some pictures while you are here," said Daddy one morning at the breakfast table.

"May I take them with my camera?" asked Danny.

"Yes, I think that will be all right," Mother said with a smile.

Later in the morning Grandfather and Grandmother posed in front of Danny's and Susan's house. Then Danny snapped the picture.

"Now, be sure to turn the film in your camera," said Mother, "before you take another picture."

Danny turned and turned, but nothing seemed to happen.

"Here, let me look at it," said Mother. "Maybe I

can find the number." She too tried to turn the film. "Why, son," she said, "you don't have any film in this camera. You didn't get a picture of Grandmother and Grandfather. I'm glad we noticed it before it was too late. We can still get a picture while they're here."

Danny's camera was empty just as some people's religion is empty. They go to church every Sunday and some of them even sing the hymns but their religion is empty, because they do not know the Lord Jesus as their Saviour. They think religion means going to church. They do not really know how to worship God for they do not know His Son.

If they would read God's Word they would learn that the Lord Jesus can be their Saviour. These persons need to accept the Lord Jesus Christ before it is too late.

Memory Verse: "Fight the good fight of faith, lay hold on eternal life, whereunto thou art also called, and hast professed a good profession before many witnesses" (I Tim. 6:12).

Questions: 1. Who was visiting at Danny's house?
2. What did Danny want to do?
3. Why didn't he get a picture?
4. Why was Mother glad that she noticed it?
5. What kind of religion do some people have?
6. How can we truly worship God?

Prayer Requests: Pray for your family, your friends, and your neighbors who say they are Christians but do not seem to have the joy of salvation.

42

GOD'S GARDEN

Songs: "What Can I Give Jesus?"; "He Wants Me Too"

Scripture: Deuteronomy 26:8-11

Story: Mother had given Susan and Danny some seeds. She had also given each of them some garden space. "You children may have your own garden this year," she said. "You may do anything you like with it."

Danny had remembered the missionary pledge he had made in his Sunday school class. "The money we give God," the teacher had said, "should be something we work for. If you make a missionary pledge, try to find some way to earn this money for yourself. Don't just ask your parents to give it to you."

"I'm going to use my garden for God," said Danny, as his mother showed him the place that was his. "In fact, I'm going to put a sign on it, 'God's Garden.'" Mother smiled her approval.

"I hope nobody steals from God's garden," said Danny. "That would be robbing God."

Mother told him that some people rob God by not giving Him their lives and their money.

Danny planted the radishes, carrots, beans, lettuce and tomatoes. Every day he watered his garden carefully and pulled the weeds. Before long there were little sprouts of green showing up in his garden. Oh, how Danny loved it!

"As soon as it is ready, I am going to sell the things and give all the money to God," he explained to his parents. "Look," he continued, "I painted that today," pointing to a sign at the entrance of his garden. The sign said, "This is God's garden. Please don't take anything without asking Him."

"The garden was God's, and you were His gardener," said Danny's teacher when he brought in the money and explained what he had done.

Don't rob God by not giving Him the first and the best of everything you have. It all belongs to Him.

Memory Verse: "Honor the Lord with thy substance, and with the firstfruits of all thine increase" (Prov. 3:9).

Questions: 1. What did Mother give the children?
2. What did Danny decide to do with his garden?
3. What did he decide to call it?
4. How do people rob God?
5. What did Danny put on his sign?
6. What should we give to God?

Prayer Requests: Pray that you will give to the Lord first, and always the best of what you have.

43

A GIFT FOR BRENDA

Songs: "What You Are"; "Can the World See Jesus in You?"

Scripture: I John 3:10-16

Story: Susan was invited to Brenda's birthday party. "I just hate Brenda," she said to her mother, "but guess I'll have to buy her a present."

"Susan," said Mother, very kindly, "that's being a hypocrite. A present is to show your love for someone. If you do not love Brenda, you should not give her a present."

"Oh, but I have to!" said Susan. "What would all the other girls think?"

"I think it would be best for you to wait to buy the present," said Mother.

Each day Mother sat down and talked to Susan about the love of Christ. "God loves drunkards, and God loves church people. God loves the little African, and God loves the white person. He showed His love by giving His own Son on the cross. He was not a hypocrite. He gave His gift because He truly loved us."

Each day Susan and Mother knelt, praying for Brenda. In her prayers Mother always said, "Put a real love in Susan's heart for Brenda."

By the end of the week, Susan went to buy her gift. "Mother," she said, "may I buy Brenda that beautiful doll? I just love it."

"I thought you said you were going to buy her a little handkerchief."

"Oh, Mother, that was before I loved her!" she said. "I'm glad we prayed for Brenda, because Jesus has shown me how to love her."

When Susan's package was all wrapped, she signed the card, "With all my love, and I really mean it. Susan."

Somehow she knew that she would soon be able to win Brenda to the Lord Jesus, and she did.

Memory Verse: "My little children, let us not love in word, neither in tongue; but in deed and in truth" (I John 3:18).

Questions: 1. What did Susan think about Brenda?
2. What did Mother say about this?
3. What did Mother and Susan do each day?
4. What did Susan finally buy for Brenda?
5. How did she sign the card?
6. Who can put love in our hearts for others?

Prayer Requests: Pray that God will fill your heart with love for others. Pray that you will live so that they will want to have Jesus in their hearts too.

44

BIMBO, THE SECOND

Songs: "Angry Words"; "Yield Not to Temptation"

Scripture: Matthew 7:1-5

Story: Danny had three pet turtles. Each had a name painted on its back. His favorite turtle was named "Bimbo."

"My mother's going to get me a turtle," said Kenny, who lived next door. "She's going to have a name painted on the back too."

"What are you going to call him?" asked Danny.

"I think I'll name mine 'Bimbo' too. I like that name."

Danny left his turtles and went into the house. He almost forgot about them until evening. When he went out to get them, there were only two turtles there. Bimbo was missing. He took a quick look around. "I'll bet Kenny took him," he grumbled.

In just a few minutes Kenny came running to Danny's house. "Look," he said, showing Danny a turtle.

"So you did swipe my turtle," said Danny, accusing his neighbor.

"Swipe it? This one's mine. Mother just bought it for me."

"I think you're a thief, Kenny," said Danny. "I think you swiped my turtle."

At that very moment, Danny's mother opened the back door. "Danny," she called, "there's a stray turtle running around in the basement. Would you please get him and put him with the other two?"

Danny looked at his neighbor. "Kenny," he said. "I'm sorry. I shouldn't have accused you."

"That's all right," said Kenny, "but I knew this one wasn't your Bimbo. Yours has his name painted in green, mine's in blue."

Memory Verse: "And he said unto them, Do violence to no man, neither accuse any falsely" (Luke 3:14).

Questions: 1. How many turtles did Danny have?
2. What was the name of Danny's favorite turtle?
3. What happened to Bimbo?
4. Whom did Danny accuse?
5. What did Danny say to Kenny?
6. What was the difference in the two Bimbos?

Prayer Requests: Pray that Jesus may fill your heart with His love, so that you will love your friends and neighbors and not criticize and judge them.

45

POISON IN THE JELLY-JAR

Songs: "Trust and Obey"; "Yield Not to Temptation"

Scripture: Ephesians 6:1-9

Story: Susan watched her mother put a big jar of something up on the top shelf of the cupboard.

"I don't want you to touch this," said Mother, "that's why I'm putting it up on the top shelf."

Right there and then Susan decided that some day she would climb to the top shelf of the cupboard and look at the jar.

Then the day came. Mother was downstairs doing the family washing. Danny was still asleep. Quietly Susan pushed a chair up to the cupboard and reached for the jar on the top shelf. She took it and put it down on the table. Turning the lid she opened it and looked in. It looked just like jelly. Then she read the label. In great, big, black letters it said, "RAT POISON." Just then Mother called from the basement.

"Susan," she said, "bring me the tablecloth on the dining-room table. It needs washing too."

Susan went to the other room, got the tablecloth, and took it downstairs to her mother. She forgot all about the jar of rat poison on the table.

When Danny got up, he took a piece of toast which Mother had fixed for him.

"Oh, boy, jelly!" he said, putting the knife in the jar that Susan had left on the table.

Susan cried when Danny had to be taken to the hospital to have his stomach pumped, but she knew it was the only way to get rid of the poison. Oh, how sorry she was that she had disobeyed Mother!

The Bible tells us that we are to obey our parents. When we disobey Mother and Dad, we are also disobeying God.

Memory Verse: "Children, obey your parents in all things: for this is well pleasing unto the Lord" (Col. 3:20).

Questions: 1. What did Mother say about the jar?
2. What did Susan decide to do?
3. What did she find in the jar?
4. What did Danny think it was?
5. What happened to him?
6. Whom do we disobey when we refuse to obey our parents?

Prayer Requests: Pray that you will obey your parents at all times.

46

THE GUM-BALL MACHINE

Songs: "The Song of the Soul Set Free"; "Nothing Between"

Scripture: John 8:31-36

Story: Danny waited by the gum-ball machine while his mother did some shopping in the drugstore. For a long while he looked longingly at the gum balls in the small round machine. If only he had a penny, he thought, he could get a ball of gum. He wished a red one would roll out because red was his favorite color.

Suddenly Danny had an idea. He stuck his finger up the slot to see how the gum balls dropped down. To his surprise there was a gum ball stuck in the slot. Danny bent his little finger around it. If only he could get it to drop down. He tried and tried, but the gum ball still stayed in the slot, and so did his finger. In just a few minutes Mother came.

She tried in vain to get Danny's finger out of the gum-ball machine. Before long the owner of the store came to offer his help, but nothing seemed to work. "I guess we'll just have to saw the machine in half," said the owner.

This frightened Danny. He had visions of the saw touching his finger. In just a few seconds he pulled his finger easily from the gum-ball machine.

"How did you get it out?" Mother said.

"Oh, it was easy!" said Danny. "I just straightened my finger."

On the way home Danny explained that he had his little finger hooked around the gum ball, hoping to get it out. He did not want to let go for fear of losing the gum ball.

Sometimes Christian boys and girls play with sin. They do not want to let go of sin, but they try to live for God too. This will never work. In order to live for the Lord Jesus we must let go of all known sin.

Memory Verse: "Let us lay aside every weight, and the sin which doth so easily beset us" (Heb. 12:1).

Questions: 1. Where was Danny's mother?
2. What did Danny do?
3. What happened to his finger?
4. Who tried to help him?
5. What frightened Danny?
6. What must we do with sin?

Prayer Requests: Pray that you will not secretly want or "hang on to" anything in your life that Jesus cannot bless.

47

A FALL INTO THE WELL

Songs: "My Sins Are Gone"; "None of Self"

Scripture: Romans 6:11-18

Story: Susan's and Danny's Uncle Frank was not a Christian. In fact, he was a drunkard. He did not love the Lord Jesus at all.

"I can give up drinking," he said one day, "and I think I will. I will give it up just a little at a time." But he never seemed really to give it up.

Aunt Martha told him that he needed Jesus to help him, or he would not be able to give it up at all. "Just a little at a time will never do it," she said.

Behind their big farm house was an old well. One day when Uncle Frank came home in a drunken condition, he fell right into the well. Aunt Martha heard him and ran out to help him. Then suddenly she had an idea. Quickly she threw a rope to him. She pulled him up a little way and then loosened the rope. Of course he fell back down again. She did this one time after the other. Uncle Frank became very angry.

"You're doing this on purpose," he shouted. "Now, get me up."

Aunt Martha smiled. "I am doing just what you say you will do about your drinking," she said. "I am pulling you up just a little at a time. Every time you fall back I pull you up again."

It was not long until Uncle Frank gave up drinking altogether. He knew that he could not do it by himself, so he asked the Lord Jesus to come into his heart to be his Saviour and take away this terrible habit.

"And, dear Lord," he prayed, "don't do it just a little at a time. Do it once and for all."

Memory Verse: "If the Son therefore shall make you free, ye shall be free indeed" (John 8:36).

Questions: 1. Who was not a Christian?
2. What did he say about his drinking?
3. What did Aunt Martha tell him?
4. What happened when Uncle Frank came home?
5. What did Aunt Martha do?
6. What did Uncle Frank finally decide?

Prayer Requests: Pray that you will give yourself completely to the Lord.

48

THE ESCAPED PRISONER

Songs: "Make Me a Blessing"; "Love the World Through Me"

Scripture: Galatians 6:1-9

Story: Everybody in town was excited. A prisoner had escaped from the penitentiary. All the policemen were called on duty. Detectives were sent out, and roadblocks were set up on all the highways. Danny's mother and father listened to the radio carefully to get the news.

"A dangerous prisoner has escaped from the prison," stated the announcer. "Warnings are being sent out all over the country. We will not be satisfied until he is back behind prison bars."

After some time the radio announcer gave another news report. "The prisoner has been captured. He is back in the prison. Everyone is safe again."

Sometimes a Christian falls into sin. This should alert other Christians. They should all be looking for this one Christian who backslid. We should pray for him but should not criticize him. We should love him and try to help him to get back into the things of the Lord. We should not gossip about him, but we should talk with him and pray for him, asking the Lord Jesus to bring this Christian back into the fold.

Do you know any Christian boys and girls who are not living for Jesus? Do you talk about them and gossip about them? Wouldn't it be better to ask the Lord Jesus to speak to their hearts and bring them back again? Then ask the Lord to help you to love them until they are back in the fold, living for the Lord Jesus again.

Memory Verse: "A new commandment I give unto you, That ye love one another; as I have loved you, that ye also love one another" (John 13:34).

Questions: 1. Why was everyone so excited?
2. What did the policemen do?
3. What did the radio announcer say?
4. What should we do when Christians fall into sin?
5. What should we not do when Christians fall into sin?
6. What should we ask the Lord to help us do?

Prayer Requests: Pray that you will not be critical or fault-finding, but loving and helpful to those who seem to be drifting from the Lord.

49

FUDGE AND CHOCOLATE CAKE

Songs: "Wonderful Words of Life"; "I Love the Old Bible"

Scripture: I Peter 2:1-4

Story: Susan's mother had just made some fudge and a chocolate cake.

"Mother," said Susan, "do you know that fudge and chocolate cake are my very favorite foods? I wish they were all I would ever have to eat."

Mother laughed. She knew that Susan would soon get sick if that were all she ate. "That would not be good for your body," said Mother.

"Oh, I'm sure it would, Mother! I could eat chocolate cake and fudge all my life. I don't think I'd ever get tired of it."

"But, honey, you need meat and potatoes and vegetables and milk," explained Mother. "Your body requires these things."

It was hard for Susan to understand this, but she listened on. "A little baby has only milk when he starts out in life, but as he grows he needs other foods, bigger portions and a heavier diet. The more he eats the more he grows. The more he grows the more he eats. But if he did not eat the right food he could not grow.

Some boys and girls think a diet of candy would be wonderful, but this could be very dangerous for it could make them very sick. Candy looks good, tastes good and smells good, but too much of it would soon make our bodies very sickly. We need to eat everything God has provided for us, so that we will become big and strong.

We need to read all of God's Word too, for that will make us strong in the Lord Jesus. Some people read only the New Testament, some the Gospel of John. But God has given us the entire Bible so that we can grow "in grace, and in the knowledge of our Lord and Saviour Jesus Christ."

Memory Verse: "It is written, That man shall not live by bread alone, but by every word of God" (Luke 4:4).

Questions: 1. What was Mother making?
2. What did Susan say about it?
3. What did Mother say our bodies needed?
4. What does a baby first eat?
5. What happens when we grow?
6. What should we do with the Bible?

Prayer Requests: Pray that as you read the Word you will take it into your life and become more like the Lord Jesus.

50

SOLDIER WITH DISEASE

Songs: "Who Is On the Lord's Side?"; "Do You Think I'll Make a Soldier?"

Scripture: II Timothy 2:1-5

Story: Susan was sitting at the piano playing "Onward Christian Soldiers." Her teacher had just given her this piece for her lesson. Daddy was listening to it. "Did you ever hear the story about the good and bad soldier?" he asked.

"No," said Susan, as she turned around on the piano bench.

"There was a wonderful soldier in the army. He went to the front lines and fought well. You see, he had an incurable disease. He knew that he would not live very long anyway, so he decided to fight his very best.

"Then something happened. A doctor in the medical corps found a certain kind of medicine and soon the soldier was cured. Suddenly, the soldier became a very poor fighter. He was afraid when he was sent to the front, and before long he was one of the worst fighters in the army.

"What happened? When the fighter was near death he did not care what happened to himself. He fought without fear. But when his body was made well he suddenly began to think about himself instead of the battle."

Sometimes when people think they have only a short time to live, they become good witnesses for Christ. Then when God heals their bodies they forget about witnessing to people. No matter what happens our concern for others cannot disappear. This would be wrong. When the Lord Jesus takes our sin away, or does some other wonderful thing for us, we should be all the more careful to give Him everything we have.

Memory Verse: "For whosoever will save his life shall lose it: and whosoever will lose his life for my sake shall find it" (Matt. 16:25).

Questions: 1. What did Daddy ask Susan?
2. What did the soldier have?
3. What did the doctor do for him?
4. Then what happened to the soldier?
5. Why did he become a poor fighter?
6. What do some Christians do when Christ heals them?

Prayer Requests: Pray that you will always be thankful to Christ for what He has done for you, so thankful that you will be concerned for others.

51

TOO FAR AWAY TO HEAR

Songs: "I'll Be Somewhere Listening"; "Jesus Is Calling"

Scripture: John 10:1-5

Story: Danny and Susan were playing in the back yard. "I'll be calling you in just a little while, so don't run away," said Mother. "I have something special I want you to do."

"Work!" grumbled Danny. "We never have any fun." The children went behind the garage. "I think it'll be all right to play here," said Susan. "We can still hear Mother's voice."

In just a few minutes Bobby Evans called from across the street. "Hey," he said, "come on over and play here."

"I guess it won't really hurt," said Danny. "We can still listen for Mother's voice." So across the street they ran.

When Bobby's mother saw them, she asked the children to come into the house for something to eat. It was then that Danny's and Susan's mother began to call, but now they could not hear her.

"I called you," said Mother when Danny and Susan finally came home. "I thought you might like to lick the fudge pan, but it's too late now. I've already washed it out." Danny and Susan moaned. Oh, how they liked to lick the fudge pan! But they had disobeyed and had not heard Mother's call.

Sometimes we sin. It does not seem very big. God calls to us and tells us it is sin. The next time we go into sin just a little bit deeper, and the third time even farther. Before long we have gone so far away that we do not hear God's call.

When we sin we must suffer for the wrong we have done. We should ask the Lord Jesus to forgive us right away. Then we should ask Him to help us so that we will not go farther into sin.

Memory Verse: "My sheep hear my voice, and I know them, and they follow me" (John 10:27).

Questions: 1. What did Mother ask of Danny and Susan?
2. What was Danny's reply?
3. Who called to the children from across the street?
4. What did they do?
5. What happened when their Mother called for them?
6. What did she have for them?

Prayer Requests: Pray that your heart may be tuned to the Lord Jesus at all times so that you will hear Him when He calls.

52

CLEANING THE SILVER

Songs: "I Washed My Hands This Morning"; "Cleanse Me"

Scripture: John 15:1-8

Story: Susan had been looking forward to dinner on this day for some time. The minister was coming to dinner today. That meant that Mother would use the best dishes, the best crystal and the best silver.

The best silver had not been used for such a long time that it had tarnished. Susan promised to help with the dinner, so she quickly took a cloth and the silver polish from the shelf and helped Mother polish the silverware. My, how beautiful it looked when she finished!

After everything was polished Susan checked each piece once again. Now she found that two forks still had spots on them. She had not rubbed hard enough to get the spots off. Since there were only going to be four at the table, Susan put the two spotted forks aside.

"We can't use anything that's not clean," she said to Mother.

The Lord is a purifier of silver too. He "casts aside" that which is not spotless. First, we need to be washed in the blood of the Lord Jesus, to have our sins forgiven, and to be born again and become children of God. Then when we are His children He purges us so that we may be clean and pure enough to bring forth fruit. The Bible tells us that we are to be fruit bearers.

And what does Christ do with those who do not live lives that are clean enough to bear fruit? This is what the Bible says: "And every branch . . . that beareth not fruit he taketh away." Yes, He puts it aside.

We cannot be used in God's service if we are soiled Christians. Be sure that your life is clean and pure so that you can be used in God's work.

Memory Verse: "Purge me with hyssop, and I shall be clean: wash me, and I shall be whiter than snow" (Ps. 51:7).

Questions: 1. Who was coming for dinner?
2. What were they going to use?
3. What did Susan decide to do?
4. What did she do with those that were not spotless?
5. What does God do with those who are not spotless?
6. What happens if we are soiled Christians?

Prayer Requests: Pray that you will know the Word of God which makes clean vessels, fit for the Master's use.

53

"CHEWING" THE BIBLE

Songs: "Take Time to Be Holy"; "More About Jesus"

Scripture: Psalm 1

Story: Danny overslept one morning, and had to hurry to get ready for school. Quickly he put on his clothes, brushed his teeth, combed his hair, and then ran downstairs.

"I'm late, Mother," he said. "I can't eat any breakfast."

"But you must have something to eat," said Mother. "Here, I'll have it ready for you right away."

Danny stuffed his mouth with a homemade roll, took a gulp of milk, and ran out of the house with his school books under his arm. At school he slumped down in his desk. Somehow he didn't feel well. He had been in such a hurry that he had not taken time to chew his food.

"I think I swallowed it whole," he said to his teacher when he explained why he was sick.

Many Christians are like Danny. They open their

Bibles hurriedly in the morning. Quickly they read a short verse. They hardly look to see what it is. Then they run. Children run to school, fathers run to work, and mothers run to household duties, and often forget to "chew" the food from God's Word.

The Bible says we should "meditate" on it day and night. That is the same as chewing. Did you take time to digest your spiritual food today? Did you "chew" it; that is, meditate or think upon it? You must not swallow your food whole.

Memory Verse: "My meditation of him shall be sweet: I will be glad in the Lord" (Ps. 104:34).

Questions: 1. What happened to Danny one morning?
2. What did he do with his breakfast?
3. What happened when he arrived at school?
4. Why was he sick?
5. What do some Christians do with their Bible reading?
6. What should we do with God's Word?

Prayer Requests: Pray to your heavenly Father that you will take time each day to read your Bible and meditate on it.

54

GOD WANTED BROTHER

Songs: "Does Jesus Care?"; "Children of the Heavenly Father"

Scripture: I Thessalonians 4:13-18

Story: Susan's and Danny's little baby brother had just died. Mother tried hard not to cry, but Susan and Danny saw the tears trickle down her cheeks all day long. Father was real quiet too. Danny and Susan just could not understand why Mother and Daddy had prayed, "Thank you, Lord, for taking our baby, Billy."

"I don't like God," said Danny, before he realized what he said.

"Oh, yes, you do, honey!" said Mother.

"But He took our baby," complained Danny.

Susan agreed. "I don't think God was nice to take our baby," she cried. "I loved him, and I didn't want God to take him away. I wanted him."

Mother took Susan in her arms and pushed back her hair. Daddy put Danny in his lap. "Children," said Daddy, "the Lord gave us our little baby. He let us have him in our house for a time. He wanted us to take care of him for a little while. Then the day came when God wanted him back. You see everything belongs to God. He just lets us use it. When He is ready He calls for it, and we must be willing to give it up. Your little baby brother was not well when he lived here. You wouldn't want him to be sick all the time, would you?"

Susan and Danny shook their heads. They did not want their little brother to be sick, but somehow they did not want him to die either. But Daddy explained that in Heaven he would never be sick again.

"I guess God was right," admitted Susan, after she had thought about it.

"Yes," said Daddy, " 'the Lord gave, and the Lord hath taken away; blessed be the name of the Lord.' "

Memory Verse: "The eternal God is thy refuge, and underneath are the everlasting arms" (Deut. 33:27).

Questions: 1. Who had just died?
2. How did Danny and Susan feel about this?
3. How did Daddy explain Billy's death?
4. Why had he died?
5. Whose baby was Billy?
6. Who gives and who takes?

Prayer Requests: Pray that you will live so close to the Lord that you will not be rebellious if He takes your loved ones to be with Him.

55

THE PLANTED WRISTWATCH

Songs: "Life Begins"; "Christ Liveth in Me"

Scripture: Matthew 13:3-8

Story: Susan's and Danny's cousin, Jimmy, was visiting them. He was only five. He watched his aunt plant something in the ground. First, she dug a hole, then she put the bulb into the ground and covered it with good fresh dirt.

"There," she said, "now we'll have lots of pretty flowers."

Jimmy wrinkled up his forehead and thought. If you can plant one flower and get lots of flowers, why not do that with everything?

"Does everything grow?" he asked.

"Everything that has life," his aunt replied.

Soon Jimmy had an idea. He looked at his aunt's wrist watch on the table. In just a few minutes he was outside digging a hole.

"There," he said, after he put the wrist watch in the dirt and covered up the hole, "now we'll have a bunch of wrist watches."

"What are you doing, Jim?" asked Danny.

"Just plantin' somethin'."

"What?" insisted Danny.

"A wrist watch," Jimmy replied.

"You can't plant a wrist watch," said Danny. "It won't grow."

Jimmy thought he would have lots of little wrist watches by planting one, but the wrist watch had no life. It could not send out roots. It would never grow. Some people go to church and think they will become better people, but unless they have eternal life they will always be sinners and never ready for Heaven.

Memory Verse: "Therefore if any man be in Christ, he is a new creature" (II Cor. 5:17).

Questions: 1. What did Jimmy's aunt plant?
2. What idea did Jimmy get?
3. What did Danny do?
4. Why wouldn't the watch grow?
5. Does everyone who goes to church belong to the Lord?
6. What must we have to be able to go to Heaven?

Prayer Requests: Pray that your life may be "planted" in the Lord Jesus, and that you will bear fruit for Him.

56

THE TEACHER'S SACRIFICE

Songs: "On the Cross for Me"; "Everybody Ought to Love Jesus"

Scripture: Isaiah 53:3-10

Story: Danny thought he could listen to stories all day long. He liked stories of heroism, especially the one Daddy was telling him now.

"A group of boys went to the park with their Sunday school teacher. After they had eaten their picnic lunch, they decided to go and explore the picnic grounds. Just around the other side of the park there was a river. The teacher warned the boys not to walk too close to the river, for it had rained heavily only a few days before and the water was high. As the boys began to explore, the teacher walked close behind the boys, trying to keep an eye on all of them. Every now and then he would call to them, 'Be careful. If you fall in that river, the waters will wash you downstream.'

"All at once one of the boys had an idea. He decided it would be safe if all the boys held hands as they walked along the narrow path. So they did.

"And then it happened. In a quick moment the

first boy lost his footing. Since all the boys were holding hands, he pulled the others into the water with him.

"Without a moment's thought, the teacher threw off his coat, jumped into the river and rescued the boys, one at a time. As he brought the last boy to shore, the teacher collapsed, fell back into the water and was drowned.

"He had given his own life in order to save the lives of these young boys."

The Lord Jesus gave His life for the entire world. "He died on the cross to save us from sin." So "everybody ought to love Jesus."

Have you accepted Him as your personal Saviour? Remember, He gave His life for you. He wants to be your Saviour today.

Memory Verse: "Greater love hath no man than this, that a man lay down his life for his friends. Ye are my friends, if ye do whatsoever I command you" (John 15:13, 14).

Questions: 1. What kind of stories did Danny like?
2. With whom were the boys?
3. Of what did he warn them?
4. What happened to one of the boys?
5. What did the teacher do?
6. Who gave His life for the whole world?

Prayer Requests: Thank God for giving His only begotten Son for you and for the whole world. Ask the Lord to save you from sin, if you have not done so.

57

A BRAVE SOLDIER

Songs: "I Gave My Life for Thee"; "I Love Him Better Every Day"

Scripture: John 3:14-18

Story: Susan and Danny were listening to the message the pastor was bringing in the morning service. Sometimes church seemed sort of long, but today it did not. The pastor was telling the story of a dying soldier, and Danny was very interested. He liked stories about soldiers, especially when it was about a brave soldier. The soldier the pastor talked about was very brave, so Danny listened carefully.

"A young sergeant, seeing an enemy pointing a rifle directly at his captain, threw himself in the way. The bullet struck the young sergeant rather than his captain. The young sergeant fell to the ground immediately, and in a few seconds he was dead. He had given his life for his captain."

Do you think the captain was grateful? I think so. Do you think he said "Thank you" to this boy's parents? I'm sure he did. Do you think he appreciated what the sergeant had done for him? Of course he did!

Jesus, God's only begotten Son, gave His life too. He gave His life because of our sins. He knew that all sin must be punished. We should have died for our sins. But instead Jesus took the blame. He was put on the cross. There He was punished for us. Shouldn't we say "Thank you" to Him? Shouldn't we tell the heavenly Father that we are grateful? Shouldn't we love Christ more? That is what the real Christian should do. I am sure that is what you will want to do too.

Memory Verse: "I lay down my life . . . No man taketh it from me, but I lay it down of myself" (John 10:17,18).

Questions: 1. Where were Danny and Susan?
2. What was the pastor talking about?
3. What did the sergeant do when the enemy came?
4. What happened to the sergeant?
5. How do you think the captain felt?
6. Who gave His life for us?

Prayer Requests: Pray that you will realize that Jesus gave His life so that you could be set free from sin.

58

NOT TOO YOUNG FOR GIFTS

Songs: "Too Small"; "I Don't Have To Wait"

Scripture: Mark 10:13-16

Story: Susan had brought another girl with her to Sunday school. The teacher was giving the lesson. She was telling the children that God's gift to us was the Lord Jesus. Then she asked all the children to bow their heads, for she was going to pray.

"Before I pray," she said, "is there someone here who would like to accept the Lord Jesus as Saviour today?"

Susan peeked just a little. "Why don't you?" she whispered to her friend.

Her friend replied, "I'm too young."

"Oh, no! You're not too young," said Susan.

After prayer, the teacher talked with both of them.

"I have some presents in my purse," she said. "I could give them to you, and I think you would like them. They would make you very happy."

Susan's friend smiled. I would like a present," she said.

"But aren't you too young to have a present?" asked the teacher.

Susan's friend laughed. "Oh, no! I would know what a present is. I would be very happy for it. I would say 'Thank you' for the present too."

Susan's teacher began to explain the way of salvation again. She said, "You are not too young to accept God's free gift. He is offering Jesus to you just as I am offering you this gift. All you need to do is accept Him as your Saviour. Just tell Him that you are a sinner, and that you believe He will take your sin away."

Susan's friend looked up at the teacher. "Is that all?" she asked.

"That's all," said the teacher. "Then you will be God's child. You will have accepted His free gift."

Together, Susan, her friend and the teacher knelt as the little girl accepted Jesus and received God's free gift.

Memory Verse: "For the wages of sin is death; but the gift of God is eternal life through Jesus Christ our Lord" (Rom. 6:23).

Questions: 1. Whom did Susan bring to Sunday school?

2. What lesson was the teacher giving?

3. What did Susan ask her friend?

4. What was her friend's answer?

5. What did the teacher offer the girl?

6. When are we old enough to accept Jesus?

Prayer Requests: Pray that when the Lord speaks to your heart you will receive His gift of eternal life.

59

THE RIGHT BLOOD

Songs: "There Is a Fountain"; "Nothing but the Blood"

Scripture: I Peter 1:18-23

Story: Linda was very sick. She had to have an operation on her heart. Linda and her mother lived next door to Danny and Susan.

"Please, Lord," prayed Daddy that night, "provide the right type of blood for Linda when she has this operation, so that she will soon be well and strong again. Amen."

The next morning Linda was taken to the hospital. Many of the neighbors went with her. They were there to volunteer as blood donors. Daddy and Mother went too. Before long, most of the people came home, but Daddy stayed.

"Where is Daddy?" asked Susan.

"He's at the hospital, honey. He's going to give blood to Linda."

"Why didn't other people give their blood?"

Mother explained that Linda needed a certain type of blood, and that just anybody's blood would not do. "Daddy had the right kind of blood and he is willing to give some of it to Linda," said Mother.

Sin is a serious heart condition too. There is only one type of blood that can change our sinful hearts and make them clean. It is the blood of the Lord Jesus. Nothing else can do this. God's Son, the Lord Jesus, gave His life on the cross. There He shed His blood. Now we can have sin taken away from our hearts and lives. Have you accepted the Lord Jesus as your Saviour? Have you accepted His sacrifice on Calvary's cross? He gave His blood so that you could live.

Linda would never have rejected the blood that she needed so much. You should not reject the blood of the Lord Jesus for your life.

Memory Verse: "In whom we have redemption through his blood, even the forgiveness of sins' (Col. 1:14).

Questions: 1. Who was sick?
2. What was to be done to her?
3. What did she need?
4. What did the neighbors do?
5. Whose blood matched Linda's?
6. Whose blood can take away our sin?

Prayer Requests: Thank the Lord Jesus for shedding His blood for you and for all the people of the world.

60

MEETING THE GOVERNOR

Songs: "Thanks to God"; "A Thank-You Song"

Scripture: Luke 17:11-19

Story: Susan and Danny were visiting their cousin, Mary Ann. Mary Ann lived right across the street from the Governor. They hoped they would get to see the Governor while they were there.

Every day the Governor would pass Mary Ann's house and stop to talk with her. Sometimes he would give her little trinkets and presents.

Susan and Danny were impressed to think that their cousin knew the Governor, and that he stopped to talk with her, and sometimes even gave her presents. One day as the Governor walked by Mary Ann's house, she introduced Susan and Danny to him. They were so thrilled that they decided they would tell everybody in school about this when they got back home. Just think, they had met a very great and important person.

We know Someone who is even greater than the Governor. He is the Lord Jesus Christ. He is the King of all kings. This very important Someone takes time to help us and take care of us. He loves us. He loves us so much that He took time to come down and die for us.

The Governor gave Mary Ann gifts, but Jesus gave us the greatest gift of all—eternal life. He has also given us mothers and fathers, homes and churches, food and rest.

Mary Ann knew her cousins would want to meet the Governor, so she introduced her cousins to Him. Have you told anyone about Jesus? Your friends will want to know Jesus too. Help them to meet Him today.

Mary Ann was always careful to say "Thank you" to the Governor whenever he gave her a gift. Have you said "Thank you" to God's only Son, the King of all kings, for dying for your sins?

Memory Verse: "Thanks be unto God for his unspeakable gift" (II Cor. 9:15).

Questions: 1. Where did Mary Ann live?
2. What did the Governor do each day?
3. What did Mary Ann do for Susan and Danny?
4. What did Susan and Danny decide to do?
5. Who is greater than a Governor?
6. What should we do for people who do not know Christ?

Prayer Requests: Pray that just now you will realize how precious the Lord Jesus is, and thank God for giving His Son to die for everyone.